MY HAND IN *Yours*

OUR HANDS IN *His*

7 - Week Marriage Workbook (Virtues)

Kimberly Cook

My Hand In *Yours* Our Hands In *His*
7 - Week Marriage Workbook (Virtues)

OUTLINE

HOW TO USE THIS STUDY

→ Take your time reading and digesting the introduction, discussing with your spouse what you hope to gain from the study and what you are willing to put into it (time, effort, commitment).

→ The study can be spread out over six (20 - 60 minute) evenings with your spouse, or you may choose to set aside just a few nights, spending more time to cover a greater amount of material.

→ Begin each section praying the provided opening prayer together, and pray the closing prayer upon concluding each study.

→ Each of the seven sections focuses on a different virtue and is separated into a study night, and three exercises:

> **Study Night** – Summarizing how that virtue is particularly relevant in our marriage

> **Exercise One** – Comprised of three questions, easily spread out over three nights

> **Exercise Two** – Discussion night, examining areas of our marriage where this virtue is plentiful and areas where it is sparse.

> **Exercise Three** – Reflection night, concluding the study week with concrete actions to institute in our marriage

If at any time you need further assistance, you can contact me at Kimberly@TheLionOfDesign.com

INTRODUCTION

Dear Married Couples,

Thank you for joining me on this journey through the virtues, which is specifically tailored toward married couples, seeking to grow spiritually with one another. The sacrament of matrimony is one of the least understood, honored, and protected vocations in our world. Yet marriage was instituted by God himself, it is the fabric of society, and marriage brings forth eternal beings in dignity. Marriage is worth pursuing and worth fighting for. As you grow in virtue with one another through this study, I hope that you will also encounter this same passion to fight for the salvation of your spouse – all the way until eternal glory!

Here are some key words/phrases to remember when bringing to mind your own marriage – covenant, lifelong partnership, ordered toward the good, holy offspring, sacrament. These are certainly some heavy-hitters, not to be taken lightly. The more we associate these words with our own marriage, the greater our respect for our vocation will be - as elevated by Christ. A holy marriage is inseparable from Christ, who laid his life down for his bride; the Church.

The focus of this marriage workbook is on the virtues, and therefore it is meant to help you and your spouse grow with one another, by incorporating the four cardinal (human) and three theological (from God) virtues into your marriage. Each of the seven weeks is devoted to a deeper knowledge of each virtue. You and your spouse should set aside three to six nights each week to work through the exercises together, revisiting them more frequently if desired. This may especially be the case if one of the exercises requires more time and deeper conversation for you, because of the state of current growth and struggle in your marriage.

The 2nd Century Christian writer Tertullian wrote this of marriage: "How can I ever express the happiness of a marriage joined by the Church, strengthened by an offering, sealed by a blessing, announced by angels, and ratified by the Father? . . . How wonderful the bond between two believers, now one in hope, one in desire, one in discipline, one in the same service! They are both children of one Father and servants of the same Master, undivided in spirit and flesh, truly two in one flesh. Where the flesh is one, one also is the spirit."[1] What profound words!

Sincerely,
Kimberly Cook

OPENING PRAYER

Lord, you have blessed us with an intellect and will to govern our actions and inspire us to pursue the good. Please help us to strive each day anew, to seek your face and grow with one another on the path toward participation in your divine nature.

You have also given us special graces in the theological virtues of faith, hope, and charity. These heavenly gifts give life to the moral virtues, helping us in all ways to receive eternal life.

Strengthen and bless our marriage and family, oh Heavenly Father, and increase our desire to know, love, and serve you more fully.

CLOSING PRAYER

Lord, give us your peace as we conclude our study together this day. Help us to choose one another before ourselves, and to embrace our daily sacrifices with joy and perseverance.

Lead us to a deeper love for one another and for others, through our constant perfection of the cardinal virtues - of prudence, justice, fortitude, and temperance.

Guide us in marriage, so that we may be a living witness of faith to the world of the goodness of this sacramental covenant. Come to our assistance when we fall, and strengthen us to forgive one another and bear each other's burdens together.

Lord, you created us out of love. Let our mutual love for one another be an image of the absolute and unfailing love with which you love us.

WEEK ONE – PRUDENCE

Study: What is Prudence in Marriage?

Prudence is definitely a great place to start in examining the virtues, as it is the guide of all other virtues. Prudence is the steering wheel that guides the ship through the rough waters of sin and temptation. The virtue of prudence can be understood as having reason and using it properly. In preventing foolish decisions, which would ultimately bring trouble, avoiding hardship, and most importantly - avoiding final damnation.

In marriage, we might practically think about prudence as the virtue which helps us, as a couple, to achieve that which brings goodness and to avoid that which brings pain and destruction. Surely, every person in his right mind wants to achieve what is good and to avoid what is bad. In its simplest form, prudence is obvious. It is easily understood through its consequences in the natural and created order. Yet, many of us struggle with *choosing* the good, regardless of our awareness of it.

Perhaps in your own marriage there have been very big moments when you or your spouse did not choose what was prudent. If so, you're in good company. Often the evil that results from the lack of prudence creates a severing of our relationship. We see this in our relationship with God, and in our need to repair that relationship through a contrite confession and penance. The break in our relationship with God is caused by us; his sons and daughters. Our first parents - Adam and Eve, had to leave the garden of Eden after severing their relationship with God through disobedience. This also happens in marriage, when our lack of prudence allows us to choose something that will inevitably hurt both our spouse and God.

God created marriage as a holy vocation, designed to bring the family into heaven, through the love of Christ. The two of you are first meant to help get one another to heaven! This is certainly not always easy. Take for example, how difficult it might be to forgive one another for past hurts. Just remember that forgiveness is the greatest gift you can give your spouse (and yourself). Forgive often, without keeping score.

If you and your spouse are both willingly sitting down to do this study together, then you are in a beautiful place, regardless of the faults currently separating you.

WEEK ONE – PRUDENCE

Exercise One - Scripture

So, let's enter into the hardest part of this exercise. Remember, the more you dig in, the more growth can occur. Also, some of the divisive moments in your marriage may have already been discussed and dealt with at some length in the past. If this is your case, you may choose not to focus on these moments again. In any case, each spouse needs to primarily ask the question, "What can I do to help myself and my spouse grow in virtue" – and not what my spouse can do for me.

    1.) Leading a morally good life brings joy. Read _Proverbs 14_ (RSVCE) out loud together. Write down and then discuss how the virtue of prudence is demonstrated again and again in this verse.

Husband:_____
_____
_____
_____
_____
_____
_____
_____

Wife:_____
_____
_____
_____
_____
_____
_____
_____

WEEK ONE – PRUDENCE

2.) Read the verse again silently, considering what line(s) specifically speaks to you of the way your spouse properly exercises the virtue of prudence in your marriage and family life together. Write down that line and a few thoughts you would like to share with them.

Husband:_____
_____
_____
_____
_____
_____
_____
_____
_____

Wife:_____
_____
_____
_____
_____
_____
_____
_____
_____

Now take turns sharing the line(s) you chose, and explain to your spouse why you chose these words to describe them, and how you see that he/she properly exercises the virtue of prudence in your marriage.

WEEK ONE – PRUDENCE

3.) Now turning the focus on myself, take a few silent moments to consider what area(s) of my life I find myself most in need of the virtue of prudence? How might my spouse be able to help me (pray specifically for this intention, support me, or something more concrete, such as removing cable or internet from the home because of distraction or temptation)?

Husband:_____
_____
_____
_____
_____
_____
_____
_____

Wife:_____
_____
_____
_____
_____
_____
_____
_____

Take turns honestly and openly sharing your conclusions with your spouse, as well as ways you might be able to help one another grow in this virtue. Make a commitment to pray daily for your spouse's intentions, and to follow up on their requests to support them.

WEEK ONE – PRUDENCE

Exercise Two - Discussion

Question: How are we living out the virtue of Prudence in Marriage?

In the first part of this exercise, we studied **Proverbs 14**, focusing on the virtue of prudence – particularly as it relates to our own marriage. We recognized the goodness of our spouse regarding this virtue, and recognized areas in our own faith journey, in which we need to grow in the virtue of prudence.

Hopefully this is a great help in starting the conversation in your marriage, and in leading one another to a greater level of prudence through holy spousal love.

Discuss:

How are we living out the virtue of prudence in our marriage? Do we give when we can, and hold back when necessary? Below are some suggestive topics in regards to living out the virtue of prudence in our marriage.

Topics:

→ **Finances** – Are we giving when we can, to worthy and charitable causes, that we both agree upon? Are we saving when its necessary and being frugal with our money? Are we buying quality and not quantity? Do we feel in control of our spending habits?

→ **Children** – Are we open to welcoming children into our marriage and family at this time, or are there valid factors necessitating us to be vigilant about not conceiving - according to the wisdom and guidance of the Church? Do we give of ourselves lovingly and generously to our children?

→ **Order**– Are we happy with the structure of our family life, or are we barely getting through each day? Do we set aside adequate time to pray, study/be creative, and exercise? If not, are there any feasible ways to remedy some of these things?

→ **Discipline** – Are we disciplined people; putting God first, spouse second, children third, and self last? How well do we plan in our marriage (spending, saving, raising children, travel, time management)? Are we prudent with waking up and going to bed at a reasonable time? Do we respect our spouse in our time management, preparation, awareness of our spouse's needs, and communicating our thoughts and plans regularly with them?

WEEK ONE – PRUDENCE

Exercise Three - Reflection

Action: How can we grow in the virtue of Prudence in our Marriage?

Every couple desires a happy marriage, and happiness in turn requires pursuing the good. Each virtue is a pursuit of some good, and requires human action and grace. St. Thalassios the Libyan said, "Blessed stillness gives birth to blessed children: self-control, love and pure prayer."[2] Do we embrace this blessed stillness?

Going forth from this study, let's reflect on how we can pray with and for one another, and what actions we can take to grow with one another in the virtue of prudence.

In regards to the discussion topics from the last exercise, what choices are we making in our marriage that we agree upon, and how are these choices helping us grow together in prudence?

_____

_____

_____

_____

_____

_____

_____

Perhaps some of the discussion topics from the last exercise are leading us further away from God and one another. What concrete actions are we going to take to remedy some of the most flawed and divided areas of exercising prudence in our marriage?

_____

_____

_____

_____

_____

_____

_____

Notes & Resolutions

WEEK TWO – JUSTICE

Study: What is Justice in Marriage?

"For I the Lord love justice," says Isaiah 61:8. Many of us can say that we love justice – it's certainly in our nature. But do we understand the depth of this virtue, particularly in regards to what is expected of us by God?

Scripture speaks of justice many times. We are called to be just and righteous. We are to care about the poor, but not to show partiality or favoritism to either the poor or the great. We must judge fairly. In other words, we should always be just to those around us - regardless of their state in life, and regardless of the honor and pride it may bring us. The virtue of justice is something that we have to cultivate within ourselves, until it comes naturally. Often, it's hard to remain blind to the irrelevant conditions that sway our judgement.

Scripture tells us that true justice requires kindness and mercy (Zechariah 7:9). Does justice look like this in our marriage? Do we will the good of our spouse at all times? Do we seek to help their spiritual and moral life flourish? Are we helping our spouse to love God first and above all else?

Justice goes far beyond rights, and it certainly doesn't involve periods of the silent treatment or intentional isolation in the home. Spouses should address the proper place of God in all decisions. Is the end goal good, and the means of achieving that goal also good? Sometimes the answer is no. The ends do not justify the means, which may have become clouded and disordered. Perhaps it's an end or goal (job, house, money, position, task, desire) that's bringing us farther away from God, and introducing other temptations into our marriage along the way.

Justice respects the human dignity of all people, especially our spouse. Two people living this abundant covenanted generosity with one another is a great testimony to the rest of the world. Through marriage, justice is exemplified and restored. From this, children grow up in households of love, properly understanding how to love God and others.

WEEK TWO – JUSTICE

Exercise One - Scripture

Justice indicates a relationship with another person, as it implies equality. St. Thomas Aquinas defines the virtue of justice as that which first requires an act of the will, and therefore is voluntary (fake it till you make it). After that, the act must be constant and perpetual.[3]

   1.) The Lord blesses the just. Read _Isaiah 61:8-9_ (RSVCE) out loud together. Write down and then discuss the blessings given to the faithful (recompense, everlasting covenant, descendants and offspring, recognition). In what ways is our marriage outwardly seen as a witness? Do people see us as blessed?

Husband:_____
_____
_____
_____
_____
_____
_____
_____

Wife:_____
_____
_____
_____
_____
_____
_____
_____

WEEK TWO – JUSTICE

2.) St. Thomas More is regarded for his excellence in the virtue of justice. In 1535 he was beheaded by King Henry VIII for remaining faithful to the Church teaching on divorce, and refusing to sign a recognition of the King's authority as head of the church. Despite much counsel advising him to sign the King's descent; in the spirit of peace and solidarity, More's conscience would not permit this injustice. His signature would have been false, and would be an assault on the true authority of the Church, of which God instituted himself. More left behind his wife and children, to die for this truth.

In what ways has my spouse been just - in rejecting to do something that may have had a good end goal, but would have been done for the wrong reasons (or was not best for our family)? On the other hand, how has my spouse been just in choosing to do something in marriage that was for our good, remaining constant and perpetual in that choice?

Husband:_____
_____
_____
_____
_____
_____
_____
_____

Wife:_____
_____
_____
_____
_____
_____
_____
_____

How has this proper exercise of the virtue of justice enhanced our marriage?

WEEK TWO – JUSTICE

3.) Now turning the focus on myself, take a few silent moments to consider what area(s) of my life I find myself most in need of the virtue of justice? How might my spouse be able to help me (pray specifically for this intention, support me in being just and defend me when my stance is challenged, regularly help to evaluate decisions before a commitment is made, help me to weigh the value of my time, talents, and treasure)?

Husband:_____
_____
_____
_____
_____
_____
_____
_____

Wife:_____
_____
_____
_____
_____
_____
_____

Take turns honestly and openly sharing your conclusions with your spouse, as well as ways you might be able to help one another grow in this virtue. Make a commitment to pray daily for your spouse's intentions, and to follow up on their requests to support them.

WEEK TWO – JUSTICE

Exercise Two - Discussion

Question: How are we living out the virtue of Justice in Marriage?

In the first part of this exercise, we studied *Isaiah 61:8-9*, focusing on the virtue of justice – particularly as it relates to our own marriage. We recognized the goodness of our spouse regarding this virtue, and recognized areas in our own faith journey, in which we need to grow in the virtue of justice.

Hopefully this is a great help in starting the conversation in your marriage, and in leading one another to a greater level of justice through holy spousal love.

Discuss:

How are we living out the virtue of justice in our marriage? Do I give God his due first (through prayer and worship), my spouse next, and myself last? Below are some suggestive topics in regards to living out the virtue of justice in our marriage.

Topics:

→ **Time** – Am I being just with my time; setting aside time to pray alone and with my family? Are the ways in which I spend my free time wholesome, and do I set aside free time to spend with my spouse?

→ **Participation** – Do I work to uphold the rights and dignity of those around me, through community involvement, politics, or parish missions?

→ **Habit** - Do I work to produce consistent and morally upright habits, such as attending mass, regular prayer, and reading scripture? Am I exemplifying justice to my family by habitually preparing myself to do what is right in every situation?

→ **Example** – Do I strive to lead by example - a life of justice; at home, in the workplace, among friends? Am I able to stand up for what is right and to challenge others on what is wrong?

WEEK TWO – JUSTICE

Exercise Three - Reflection

Action: How can we grow in the virtue of Justice in our Marriage?

Every couple desires a happy marriage, and happiness in turn requires pursuing the good. Each virtue is a pursuit of some good, and requires human action and grace.

Going forth from this study, let's reflect on how we can pray with and for one another, and what actions we can take to grow with one another in the virtue of justice.

In regards to the discussion topics from the last exercise, in what areas of our marriage can we agree that we are making the most progress, and how are these choices helping us to grow together in justice?

_____
_____
_____
_____
_____
_____
_____

Perhaps some of the discussion topics from the last exercise are leading us further away from God and one another. What concrete actions are we going to take to remedy some of the most flawed and divided areas of exercising justice in our marriage?

_____
_____
_____
_____
_____
_____
_____

Notes & Resolutions

WEEK THREE – FORTITUDE

Study: What is Fortitude in Marriage?

Fortitude is the virtue I am convinced we are most in need of in marriage, or in any state of life for that matter! Fortitude keeps us firmly rooted in Christ and in the duties of our vocation, especially in difficult situations or periods of time.

The virtue of fortitude helps us to constantly pursue the good, and to avoid temptations. Often Christians remark that they cannot imagine how couples remain married without the direction of Christ to lead and guide them. Sadly, we see that many do not remain married. This is also true for Christian marriages, particularly when Christ is no longer central.

As fallen men and women, we have a temptation to put ourselves above others. At times we listen to the voice of the devil, who whispers in our ear, always asking us where our reward and gratification can be found. This is dangerous because often our reward is hidden in Christ. It is found along the narrow road – through sacrifice and dying to self, many times.

What do I mean by "dying to self?" For a just cause, a good man will sacrifice anything - even his life. Christ laid his life down for each of us – the just and unjust. Looking at the sacrifices of the martyrs, sometimes we are tempted to say that we could easily suffer a quick martyrdom. But it is the daily martyrdoms we are asked to suffer, and these are the most difficult and wearing upon us.

For these daily trials and heroic moments, we need the virtue of fortitude. In preparing and cooking meals when we are tired, in waking up early on weekends with small children, in choosing our spouse over our friends or alternate entertainment, in being last instead of first, and in choosing joy instead of bitterness.

In _Romans 12:1_, St. Paul states "I appeal to you therefore, brethren, by the mercies of God, to present your bodies as a living sacrifice, holy and acceptable to God, which is your spiritual worship." This image of our bodies as a "living sacrifice" is a good way to think about the virtue of fortitude. Our Christian journey will require firmness and constancy along the way. We will most likely be living out our sacrifices day by day, rather than in an instant of saintly martyrdom.

WEEK THREE – FORTITUDE

Exercise One - Scripture

Virtues certainly require work in becoming habitual. Imagine how helpful habitual fortitude can be in choosing a difficult path bravely. Fortitude helps us act virtuously when we have foresight, as well as in the face of sudden occurrences. Scripture helps us to have this foresight.

      1.) We are living sacrifices. Read *Romans 12:1-2* (RSVCE) out loud together. Write down and then discuss the ways in which your marriage is a sacrificial witness to others. In what ways do you not allow yourselves to conform to the world, but rather to be transformed to the will of God?

Husband:_____
_____
_____
_____
_____
_____
_____
_____

Wife:_____
_____
_____
_____
_____
_____
_____
_____

WEEK THREE – FORTITUDE

Pope St. Gregory I said "The blow that is foreseen strikes with less force, and we are able more easily to bear earthly wrongs, if we are forearmed with the shield of foreknowledge."[4] This certainly doesn't mean that we can foresee all the trials and difficulties ahead of us, or that we should fear them. Rather, we should work on being virtuous, and through reason, be aware of potential trials, so that we may meet them with confidence, and find joy in the sacrifices asked of us by Christ.

2.) In what ways has my spouse born trials and difficulties in our marriage? How has she/he been a living sacrifice (bearing illness and burdens with fortitude, waking up at night with children, setting aside personal desires and choosing the desires of others in our family over her/his own)?

Husband:_____
_____
_____
_____
_____
_____
_____
_____

Wife:_____
_____
_____
_____
_____
_____
_____
_____

Take some time to share these with your spouse, and thank them for these sacrifices.

WEEK THREE – FORTITUDE

3.) Now turning the focus on myself, take a few silent moments to consider what area(s) of my life I find myself most in need of the virtue of fortitude? What are the hardest ordinary struggles and sacrifices for me in our marriage (the lack of personal time, bearing the burdens of the other, necessary periods of abstinence, coping with a mental/physical illness, indecision, extended family)?

Husband:_____
_____
_____
_____
_____
_____
_____
_____
_____

Wife:_____
_____
_____
_____
_____
_____
_____
_____

Take turns honestly and openly sharing your conclusions with your spouse, as well as ways you might be able to help one another grow in this virtue. Make a commitment to pray daily for your spouse's intentions, and to follow up on their requests to support them.

WEEK THREE – FORTITUDE

Exercise Two - Discussion

Question: How are we living out the virtue of Fortitude in Marriage?

In the first part of this exercise, we studied **Romans 12:1-2**, focusing on the virtue of fortitude – particularly as it relates to our own marriage. We recognized the goodness of our spouse regarding this virtue, and recognized areas in our own faith journey, in which we need to grow in the virtue of fortitude.

Hopefully this is a great help in starting the conversation in your marriage, and in leading one another to a greater level of fortitude through holy spousal love.

Discuss:

How are we living out the virtue of fortitude in our marriage? Do we persevere in the face of difficulty, constantly pursuing the good? Below are some suggestive topics in regards to living out the virtue of fortitude in our marriage.

Topics:

→ **Temper** – Our temper can be defined as our state of mind, particularly in stressful or uncomfortable situations. Practicing to control our temper helps us to handle our thoughts and emotions with balance. Gaining control of our temper reduces situations of regret and increases the trust our spouse and family place in us.

→ **Patience** – This is a gift of the Holy Spirit, and most of us understand why. Patience certainly seems humanly impossible at times. Yet, in order to remain firm and constant on our holy path, we must continue to pray for and perfect opportunities for patience.

→ **Expectations** – Setting proper expectations for ourselves, spouse, and children is necessary in the marathon of family life. We are often let down when we expect to accomplish more than is proper or fair to our current state and season in life. We may also find ourselves frustrated when we expect those around us to read our minds without us properly communicating our thoughts and feelings with them. Expectations must remain constant and reasonable.

WEEK THREE – FORTITUDE

Exercise Three - Reflection

Action: How can we grow in the virtue of Fortitude in our Marriage?

St. Faustina said, "I know well that the greater and more beautiful the work is, the more terrible will be the storms that rage against it."[5] Our marriage is truly a great and beautiful work!

Going forth from this study, let's reflect on how we can pray with and for one another, how we can weather the storms in our marriage better, and what actions we can take to grow with one another in the virtue of fortitude.

In regards to the discussion topics from the last exercise, in what areas of our marriage can we agree that we are making the most progress, and how are these choices helping us to grow together in fortitude?

_____
_____
_____
_____
_____
_____
_____

Perhaps some of the discussion topics from the last exercise are leading us further away from God and one another. What concrete actions are we going to take to remedy some of the most flawed and divided areas of exercising fortitude in our marriage?

_____
_____
_____
_____
_____
_____
_____

Notes & Resolutions

WEEK FOUR – TEMPERANCE

Study: What is Temperance in Marriage?

Temperance can rightly be understood as moderation. The virtue of temperance moderates restraint and excess, helping us to balance and order our marriage. Christ is our model and the Church is our example, but ultimately each of us is endowed with reason and a will - in order to moderate properly for ourselves.

The beauty of the vocation of marriage is that we have our spouse as partner and helpmate to seek the virtuous life alongside us. Together we are able to moderate decisions in our marriage and for our family.

When we entered into our marriage, moderating decisions together may have been a difficult change to adopt, especially after living alone and making all decisions in regards to temperance by ourselves. Suddenly, the way we spend our time and money (shopping, dining out, traveling, leisure), had to be discussed, limited, and considered in advance.

Temperance helps us master our instincts and desires - ordering them toward what is honorable and good. Practically, this might look like holding off on a vacation or deciding not take out a loan. Spiritually, it may require us to address issues in our marriage such as excessive drinking or a lack of love and honor for God and spouse.

Scripture tells us, "For the grace of God has appeared for the salvation of all men, training us to renounce irreligion and worldly passions, and to live sober, upright, and godly lives in this world" ~ **Titus 2:11-12**. This is not to say that we shouldn't enjoy life and take joy in created goods. Rather, created goods should rightly have their place in our lives, never ruling our passions. God should come before all else, and the way we love our spouse, our family, and all created things should be a reflection of our love of God.

WEEK FOUR – TEMPERANCE

Exercise One - Scripture

Temperance is often the nagging virtue that we want to leave us alone when we are in the midst of worldly passions. It scolds us for choosing base desires, and encourages us to turn to the Lord. St. Paul tells us that "The desires of the flesh are against the Spirit, and the desires of the Spirit are against the flesh."

1.) As Christians, we are always seeking to live by the Spirit. Read _Galatians 5:16-24_ (RSVCE) out loud together. Write down and then discuss the ways in which your marriage embraces temperance. The world hungers for healthy marriages. What gifts of the Spirit does your marriage embody, and how do these gifts express the love of Christ to others?

Husband:_____
_____
_____
_____
_____
_____
_____
_____

Wife:_____
_____
_____
_____
_____
_____
_____
_____

WEEK FOUR – TEMPERANCE

The wisdom of *Sirach 18:33* warns, "Do not become a beggar by feasting with borrowed money, when you have nothing in your purse." This is simple yet strong wisdom. The flesh sometimes desires an excess of the luxuries that the world can provide. The Spirit of God moderates with healthy discretion.

2.) In what ways has my spouse listened to the wisdom of the Holy Spirit? How has she/he embraced temperance (fought an addiction, quit a bad habit, given up a desire such as a physical item or vacation, chose a lesser house or car, sacrificed a desire for the good of self or others)?

Husband:_____

_____

_____

_____

_____

_____

_____

_____

Wife:_____

_____

_____

_____

_____

_____

_____

_____

Take some time to share these with your spouse, and thank them for their heroic efforts in listening to the Holy Spirit and embracing temperance in your marriage.

WEEK FOUR – TEMPERANCE

3.) Now turning the focus on myself, take a few silent moments to consider what area(s) of my life I find myself most in need of the virtue of temperance? What instincts, desires, and pleasures are the hardest for me to moderate (an addiction, habit, temptation, desire to spend money, need to indulge, need for recognition, procrastination, avoidance)?

Husband:_____
_____
_____
_____
_____
_____
_____
_____
_____

Wife:_____
_____
_____
_____
_____
_____
_____
_____

Take turns honestly and openly sharing your conclusions with your spouse, as well as ways you might be able to help one another grow in this virtue. Make a commitment to pray daily for your spouse's intentions, and to follow up on their requests to support them. This may also require seeking out professional counseling to resolve and repair issues.

WEEK FOUR – TEMPERANCE

Exercise Two - Discussion

Question: How are we living out the virtue of Temperance in Marriage?

In the first part of this exercise, we studied *Galatians 5:16-24*, focusing on the virtue of temperance – particularly as it relates to our own marriage. We recognized the goodness of our spouse regarding this virtue, and recognized areas in our own faith journey, in which we need to grow in the virtue of temperance.

Hopefully this is a great help in starting the conversation in your marriage, and in leading one another to a greater level of temperance through holy spousal love.

Discuss:

How are we living out the virtue of temperance in our marriage? Do we moderate restraint and excess - exercising balance? Below are some suggestive topics in regards to living out the virtue of temperance in our marriage.

Topics:

→ **Spending/Saving** - Balancing our finances is certainly an important part of marriage. Temperance helps us to moderate when to spend and when to save - with discretion. This balance often requires virtue, as well as regular spousal communication. Temptation can creep into both areas (spending for the sake of keeping up with worldly trends and desires, and saving for the sake of fear or greed).

→ **Giving/Tithing** - Are we giving back to God the first fruits of what he has blessed us with? Are we able to tithe the suggested 10% (Malachi 3:10), before considering our own wants and desires? Do we consider the poor and needy in our giving, and do we make the choice together as to where and how we will give charitably (physically, spiritually, financially)?

→ **Vigilance** – It's so easy to slip into immorality - by what we say and do, what we watch and listen to, or who we choose to hang out with. Sometimes gossip and impurity come more easily in certain situations and company. It's important to be aware of this and cautiously avoid the near occasion of sin. Perhaps this means distancing a relationship, changing jobs, and refusing certain invitations. Temperance helps us moderate unhealthy situations and stick to boundaries.

WEEK FOUR – TEMPERANCE

Exercise Three - Reflection

Action: How can we grow in the virtue of Temperance in our Marriage?

St. Teresa of Avila said, "Our body has this defect that, the more it is provided care and comforts, the more needs and desires it finds."[6] Are we ever fulfilled, or do we always desire more?

Going forth from this study, let's reflect on how we can pray with and for one another, and what actions we can take to grow with one another in the virtue of temperance.

In regards to the discussion topics from the last exercise, in what areas of our marriage can we agree that we are making the most progress, and how are these choices helping us to grow together in temperance?

_____
_____
_____
_____
_____
_____
_____

Perhaps some of the discussion topics from the last exercise are leading us further away from God and one another. What concrete actions are we going to take to remedy some of the most flawed and divided areas of exercising temperance in our marriage?

_____
_____
_____
_____
_____
_____
_____

Notes & Resolutions

WEEK FIVE – FAITH

Study: What is Faith in Marriage?

The theological virtue of faith is a heavenly gift. By the virtue of faith, and the use of reason, we believe in God and all that he has said and revealed. We know this because it is infused into our souls by God, so that we may one day come to him, of our own will, into eternal life.

God is truth itself, and all things were rightly created by God to be ordered toward this truth. When we seek what is true and good, and continue to orient ourselves toward the virtues, faith will become clear and natural to us.

Paul writes in **_Romans 1:16-17_**, "For I am not ashamed of the gospel: it is the power of God for salvation to everyone who has faith, to the Jew first and also to the Greek. For in it the righteousness of God is revealed through faith for faith; as it is written, "He who through faith is righteous shall live."'

This is interesting – Paul says the gospel reveals God "through faith for faith." Faith first takes an act of love. This act does not negate our reason or free will, but rather enhances each in fulfilling its final end – the discovery of God. In order to grow in faith, love, or any of the virtues for that matter, we must first soften our hearts and open ourselves up to God in faith.

But how are we to do this? In the same way that the father of the boy with the unclean spirit cried out to Jesus, "I believe; help my unbelief!" (Mk 9:24). This prayer moved Jesus to take pity on the man and his son, and to cast out the unclean spirit.

Faith is personal, but it is also to be shared. We are to practice it inwardly and outwardly. We are to profess it and share it with others. We are even to die for our faith, if it is required of us to do so. Jesus said this when he said "whoever denies me before men, I also will deny before my Father who is in heaven."

Spouses who are divided in faith within marriage are divided in their capacity to love – for the believer in Jesus Christ has a supernatural ability to love and forgive, beyond his own human nature. Scripture warns in both the Old and New Testament of the dangers of being united with an unbeliever. This is not to say that the love of Christ cannot overcome – for the sacramental graces work outside of human capacities. A person drawn toward truth and goodness is already on his way to God.

WEEK FIVE – FAITH

Exercise One – Marriage as an Act of Faith

Marriage is the only sacrament in which the man and woman are the ministers of the sacrament. The priest receives the consent of the spouses ("I Do") in the name of the Church, and by that authority blesses the marriage. The marriage covenant requires an act of the will by both parties, and the mutual self-giving and receiving of the other is sealed by God himself.

The marital bond is established in such a way by God that it cannot be dissolved, and in its authentic form is a participation in divine love. "In a Christian marriage the spouses are strengthened and, as it were, consecrated for the duties and the dignity of their state *by a special sacrament.*"[7]

     1.) What role does faith play in our marriage? How does proper worship of God alongside my spouse renew our marriage covenant and better prepare us for our state of married life?

Husband:_____
_____
_____
_____
_____
_____
_____
_____

Wife:_____
_____
_____
_____
_____
_____
_____
_____

WEEK FIVE – FAITH

Faith can seem paradoxical; for instance, St Augustine said, "Faith is to believe what you do not see; the reward of this faith is to see what you believe."[8] From the outside, faith may appear to be more of a mind game. Yet, marriage can be looked at through a similar lens. When we said "I Do" to our spouse, we entered into a covenant with a great deal of faith – faith in God, our self, and the other person. We could not see the graces at work, but we believed on some level that they were there.

2.) In what ways has my spouse exercised his/her faith in strengthening our marriage, and how have we seen the reward of that faithfulness through the years (children, healing, deeper prayer, sacrifice, conversions, leading others to Christ)?

Husband:_____
_____
_____
_____
_____
_____
_____
_____

Wife:_____
_____
_____
_____
_____
_____
_____
_____

Take some time to share these with your spouse, and thank them for embracing faith in your marriage.

WEEK FIVE – FAITH

3.) Now turning the focus on myself, take a few silent moments to consider what area(s) of my life I find myself most in need of the virtue of faith? When does my faith struggle and fail? When do I find myself in the most need of crying out to Jesus to help my unbelief (when I'm frustrated, tempted, suffering, struggling, unrewarded, unrecognized, anxious, hurt)?

Husband:_____
_____
_____
_____
_____
_____
_____
_____

Wife:_____
_____
_____
_____
_____
_____
_____
_____

Take turns honestly and openly sharing your conclusions with your spouse, as well as ways you might be able to help one another grow in this virtue. Make a commitment to pray daily for your spouse's intentions, and to follow up on their requests to support them.

WEEK FIVE – FAITH

Exercise Two - Discussion

Question: How are we living out the virtue of Faith in Marriage?

In the first part of this exercise, we studied **Romans 1:16-17**, focusing on the virtue of faith – particularly as it relates to our own marriage. We recognized the goodness of our spouse regarding this virtue, and recognized areas in our own faith journey, in which we need to grow in the virtue of faith.

Hopefully this is a great help in starting the conversation in your marriage, and in leading one another to a greater level of faith through holy spousal love.

Discuss:

How are we living out the virtue of faith in our marriage? Do we freely commit our entire selves to God, seeking to know and do his will? Do we recognize that only through a better relationship with Christ can we properly love one another? Below are some suggestive topics in regards to living out the virtue of faith in our marriage.

Topics:

→ **Prayer** - We must first turn toward God in prayer, asking him to increase in us the theological virtue of faith – so that our desire to know him will constantly become greater, and we can better love each other.

→ **Study** - Scripture is the first point of study in knowing God. Do we study scripture together and seek out resources to assist us in understanding it fully and correctly? As well, the saints, Church fathers, and scripture scholars through the ages have poured out wisdom of God through pages of texts. Have we set aside time to know God through these resources?

→ **Worship** – The sacraments are instituted by Christ as our life force in the Church. Without them we are weak and susceptible to sin and division. Do we attend Mass on Sundays together as a family, according to the commandments - receiving Jesus in his body, blood, soul, and divinity? Do we partake of the graces of the sacraments and encourage one another to do so frequently? Do we pray together and make our home a place of prayer and worship, as a domestic church?

WEEK FIVE – FAITH

Exercise Three - Reflection

Action: How can we grow in the virtue of Faith in our Marriage?

St. Thomas Aquinas said of faith: "To one who has faith, no explanation is necessary. To one without faith, no explanation is possible."[9]

Going forth from this study, let's reflect on how we can pray with and for one another, and what actions we can take to grow with one another in greater openness to the virtue of faith.

In regards to the discussion topics from the last exercise, in what areas of our marriage can we agree that we are making the most progress, and how are these choices helping us to grow together in faith?

_____
_____
_____
_____
_____
_____
_____

Perhaps we are lacking in some areas of the suggested discussion topics from the last exercise, and because of this we are growing further from Christ. What concrete actions are we going to take to remedy the most flawed and divided areas barring growth in faith in our marriage?

_____
_____
_____
_____
_____
_____
_____

Notes & Resolutions

WEEK SIX – HOPE

Study: What is Hope in Marriage?

The theological virtue of hope is a heavenly gift. Hope is necessary on the Christian journey, as it opposes despair and discouragement. Hope is the desire of good things to come – primarily happiness in this life and ultimately in the next.

Hope comes not through our own strength, although we can and should have the desire for this hope. We can pray for an increase in hope, and we can order all things in our lives to encourage our belief that hope is possible. Still, in the end, hope comes from God.

Look around you and see the many people living without hope. How many have given up on hope and instead embraced despair? How many spouses have lost hope in their marriage, and with it the desire to even ask for hope? The devil lives in this realm.

All of Christendom can look to the example of Abraham, who believed against hope. God made a covenant with him and promised to bless and multiply his descendants.

> In hope he believed against hope, that he should become the father of many nations; as he had been told, 'So shall your descendants be.' He did not weaken in faith when he considered his own body, which was as good as dead because he was about a hundred years old, or when he considered the barrenness of Sarah's womb. No distrust made him waver concerning the promise of God, but he grew strong in his faith as he gave glory to God, fully convinced that God was able to do what he had promised. ~ ***Romans 4:18-21***

In marriage, we must first have the hope in our own eternal salvation – salvation in Jesus Christ is true and possible, heaven does exist, and God has given us a way to attain eternal salvation. Convinced of this truth, we must live accordingly in marriage – stopping at nothing to get our spouse also to heaven.

WEEK SIX – HOPE

Exercise One – Marriage as an Act of Hope

My favorite scripture verse culminates in hope. St. Paul says in **Romans 5:2-5**, "We rejoice in our hope of sharing the glory of God. More than that, we rejoice in our sufferings, knowing that suffering produces endurance, and endurance produces character, and character produces hope, and hope does not disappoint us, because God's love has been poured into our hearts through the Holy Spirit who has been given to us."

    1.) What role does hope play in our marriage? Do we believe that hope will not disappoint us? Are we able to ask for hope, rejoice in hope, and also rejoice in suffering – knowing what it is producing in us?

Husband:_____
_____
_____
_____
_____
_____
_____
_____

Wife:_____
_____
_____
_____
_____
_____
_____
_____

WEEK SIX – HOPE

G. K. Chesterton wrote, "Fairy tales do not tell children the dragons exist. Children already know that dragons exist. Fairy tales tell children the dragons can be killed."[10] Sit back for a moment and think about that! It's an awesome statement about hope – instilling hope in children. Do we have this same childlike hope in our own marriage?

2.) In what ways does my spouse slay the dragons that creep up in our marriage? How does he/she cling to hope in every battle - big and small (pray, love deeper, give more, reach out to others for help, communicate and spend time alone even when it's difficult, allow intimacy, exercise patience)?

Husband:_____
_____
_____
_____
_____
_____
_____
_____
_____

Wife:_____
_____
_____
_____
_____
_____
_____
_____

Take some time to share these with your spouse, and thank them for embracing hope in your marriage.

WEEK SIX – HOPE

3.) Now turning the focus on myself, take a few silent moments to consider what area(s) of my life I find myself most in need of the virtue of hope? What dragons do I need to slay (frustration, guilt, temptation, a grudge, hardness of heart, animosity, despair)?

Husband:_____
_____
_____
_____
_____
_____
_____
_____

Wife:_____
_____
_____
_____
_____
_____
_____
_____

Take turns honestly and openly sharing your conclusions with your spouse, as well as ways you might be able to help one another grow in this virtue. Make a commitment to pray daily for your spouse's intentions, and to follow up on their requests to support them.

WEEK SIX – HOPE

Exercise Two - Discussion

Question: How are we living out the virtue of Hope in Marriage?

In the first part of this exercise, we studied *Romans 4:18-21*, focusing on the virtue of hope – particularly as it relates to our own marriage. We recognized the goodness of our spouse regarding this virtue, and recognized areas in our own faith journey, in which we need to grow in the virtue of hope.

Hopefully this is a great help in starting the conversation in your marriage, and in leading one another to a greater level of hope through holy spousal love.

Discuss:

How are we living out the virtue of hope in our marriage? Are we truly one in hope, regardless of how impossible the promise of God might seem? Below are some suggestive topics in regards to living out the virtue of hope in our marriage.

Topics:

→ **Wonder** - Do we wonder together – marvel, admire, and find beauty in one another, our children, creation, and God? Do we dream with one another, hoping for a future filled with joy and fulfillment?

→ **Desire** - Are our desires, goals, and hopes properly ordered within the context of faith? Do we realize that our spouse cannot fulfill these things, but only Christ? St. John Paul II said of this, "You perceive it in the depths of your heart: all that is good on earth, all professional success, even the human love that you dream of, can never fully satisfy your deepest and most intimate desires. Only an encounter with Jesus can give full meaning to your lives."[11]

→ **Suffering** – When we experience suffering, do we bear it well with one another? How have we allowed the suffering in our marriage to produce endurance, character, and hope within us?

WEEK SIX – HOPE

Exercise Three - Reflection

Action: How can we grow in the virtue of Hope in our Marriage?

Through our faithfulness to God and one another in marriage, we witness to God's faithful love to humanity. How many of us have incurred brokenness by the failed marriages of others? How can our marriage restore hope?

Going forth from this study, let's reflect on how we can pray with and for one another, and what actions we can take to grow with one another in greater openness to the virtue of hope.

In regards to the discussion topics from the last exercise, in what areas of our marriage can we agree that we are making the most progress, and how are these choices helping us to grow together in hope?

_____
_____
_____
_____
_____
_____
_____

Perhaps we are lacking in some areas of the suggested discussion topics from the last exercise, and because of this we are growing further from Christ. What concrete actions are we going to take to remedy the most flawed and divided areas barring growth in hope in our marriage?

_____
_____
_____
_____
_____
_____
_____

Notes & Resolutions

WEEK SEVEN – CHARITY

Study: What is Charity in Marriage?

The theological virtue of charity is a heavenly gift. In true charity we love God above all else, not out of fear, but rather for his own sake - because it is right and just to do so. As a child loves his parent, so God hopes to be loved by each of us.

Jesus also requires us to share this love – that we may love one another as he has loved us. In marriage, men and women share a special love, as they were created for one another since the beginning. Their union supernaturally causes the two to become one flesh.

Charity is the highest of all virtues, for without it, virtue means and gains nothing. Only through charity is our human love elevated to that of divine love. Charity animates and inspires the virtues within us, and allows us to love God as children, rather than slaves.

Love never ends! This is a reality that we strive to model and perfect in our own marriage, so that our children, as well as our neighbor, may know that God's love never ends.

Charity is difficult, as it is opposed to our fallen nature, and opposed to sin. St. Paul describes charity in _**1 Corinthians 13:4-8**_ stating, "Love is patient and kind; love is not jealous or boastful; it is not arrogant or rude. Love does not insist on its own way; it is not irritable or resentful; it does not rejoice at wrong, but rejoices in the right. Love bears all things, believes all things, hopes all things, endures all things. Love never ends."

How do we possibly love like this? How do we lay our lives down for one another like Christ did for us? How do we put ourselves last? How are we expected to endure all things? St. Thérèse of Lisieux wrote, "I feel that when I am charitable it is Jesus alone who acts in me; the more I am united to Him the more do I love all my Sisters."[12]

WEEK SEVEN – CHARITY

Exercise One – Marriage as an Act of Charity

St. Augustine said, "The *fruits* of charity are joy, peace, and mercy; charity demands beneficence (benefit of others) and fraternal correction; it is benevolence (kindness); it fosters reciprocity and remains disinterested and generous; it is friendship and communion: Love is itself the fulfillment of all our works. There is the goal; that is why we run: we run toward it, and once we reach it, in it we shall find rest."[13]

      1.) What role does charity play in our marriage? Do we have a communion of friendship that is well-intentioned and kind toward the other? Do we share the love of Christ through our love for one another, and do we exemplify his love through our holy union?

Husband:_____
_____
_____
_____
_____
_____
_____
_____

Wife:_____
_____
_____
_____
_____
_____
_____
_____

WEEK SEVEN – CHARITY

St. Josemaria Escriva said, "It is important for married people to acquire a clear sense of the dignity of their vocation. They must know that they have been called by God not only to human love but also to a divine love, through their human love. It is important for them to realize that they have been chosen from all eternity to cooperate with the creative power of God by having and then bringing up children. Our Lord asks them to make their home and their entire family life a testimony of all the Christian virtues."[14]

2.) In what ways does my spouse act for my benefit in our marriage? How does he/she love like St. Paul describes (patient, kind, not jealous or boastful, not arrogant or rude, does not insist on his/her own way, is not irritable or resentful, does not rejoice at wrong, rejoices in the right, bears all things, believes all things, hopes all things, endures all things)?

Husband:_____
_____
_____
_____
_____
_____
_____
_____
_____

Wife:_____
_____
_____
_____
_____
_____
_____
_____

Take some time to share these with your spouse, and thank them for embracing charity in your marriage.

WEEK SEVEN – CHARITY

3.) Now turning the focus on myself, take a few silent moments to consider what area(s) of my life I find myself most in need of the virtue of charity? Do I lay my life down for my spouse as the Lord asks (forgive, accept fraternal correction well, resist anger and hatred, renew my love every day)?

Husband:_____
_____
_____
_____
_____
_____
_____
_____

Wife:_____
_____
_____
_____
_____
_____
_____
_____

Take turns honestly and openly sharing your conclusions with your spouse, as well as ways you might be able to help one another grow in this virtue. Make a commitment to pray daily for your spouse's intentions, and to follow up on their requests to support them.

WEEK SEVEN – CHARITY

Exercise Two - Discussion

Question: How are we living out the virtue of Charity in Marriage?

In the first part of this exercise, we studied *1 Corinthians 13:4-8*, focusing on the virtue of charity – particularly as it relates to our own marriage. We recognized the goodness of our spouse regarding this virtue, and recognized areas in our own faith journey, in which we need to grow in the virtue of charity.

Hopefully this is a great help in starting the conversation in your marriage, and in leading one another to a greater level of charity through holy spousal love.

Discuss:

How are we living out the virtue of charity in our marriage? Do we focus on our spouse and children, bringing the same joy into our home as was found in the home of the Holy family? Below are some suggestive topics in regards to living out the virtue of charity in our marriage.

Topics:

→ **Forgiveness** - Pride is the greatest enemy of married life, and often the reason we can't forgive our spouse. But charity cannot be resentful, and if marriage is a reflection of God's love for us, then we must be willing to forgive the deepest hurts and greatest wrongs. Do we forgive?

→ **Fruitfulness**- Does our love bear good fruit? This may certainly be seen by most through children, and the richness of charity mutually poured into them. Do I also strive to bring my spouse happiness and joy through my charity toward them? Does our love and good will extend to others - that they are also being drawn into Christ's love through ours?

→ **Generosity** – Do we give to one another and to others in need, whatever is asked of us? Do we recognize that love hurts – that Christ on the cross exemplified love and suffering to the fullest? God may ask us to welcome more children into our family, or to suffer the infertility of welcoming few or none. He may ask us to give more to the poor, or require more of our time. Do we generously respond?

WEEK SEVEN – CHARITY

Exercise Three - Reflection

Action: How can we grow in the virtue of Charity in our Marriage?

Mother Teresa said, "I have found the perfect paradox, that if you love until it hurts, there can be no more hurt, only more love."[15]

Going forth from this study, let's reflect on how we can pray with and for one another, and what actions we can take to grow with one another in greater openness to the virtue of charity.

In regards to the discussion topics from the last exercise, in what areas of our marriage can we agree that we are making the most progress, and how are these choices helping us to grow together in charity?

_____
_____
_____
_____
_____
_____
_____

Perhaps we are lacking in some areas of the suggested discussion topics from the last exercise, and because of this we are growing further from Christ. What concrete actions are we going to take to remedy the most flawed and divided areas barring growth in charity in our marriage?

_____
_____
_____
_____
_____
_____
_____

Notes & Resolutions

CLOSING

Dear Married Couples,

I hope you have both greatly enjoyed this study in the virtues for married couples. I pray that it has been a useful tool to strengthen your sacramental marriage, increase dialogue and communication between you, and help you grow together in holiness and virtue.

Remember the revelation of Scripture, the guidance of the Church, and the wisdom of the saints. As Pope St. Gregory the Great said, "The only true riches are those that make us rich in virtue. Therefore, if you want to be rich, beloved, love true riches. If you aspire to the heights of real honor, strive to reach the kingdom of Heaven. If you value rank and renown, hasten to be enrolled in the heavenly court of the Angels."[16]

May you grow rich in virtue with one another and reach the heights of the heavenly courts through your vocation of marriage – leading many others to Christ through your holy witness!

If this workbook has helped your marriage, please pass it on and share it with others.

Peace and blessings,

Kimberly Cook

REFLECTIONS

References

[1] *The Catechism of the Catholic Church*, 2nd ed. (Vatican: Libreria Editrice Vaticana, 2012), para. 1642.

[2] Nikodimos and Makarios of Corinth, *The Philokalia: The Complete Text*, ed. G. E. H. Palmer, Philip Sherrard, and Kallistos Ware, Vol. 2 (London: Faber & Faber, 1866), para 83.

[3] Thomas Aquinas, *Summa Theologica* IIa-IIæ, Q. 58, Art. 1.

[4] Ibid., IIa-IIæ, Q. 123, Art. 9.

[5] Maria Faustina Kowalska, *Diary of Saint Maria Faustina Kowalska: Divine Mercy in My Soul* (Stockbridge: Marian Press, 1987), notebook V, section 1401 (37), 499.

[6] "Teresa Avila Quotes," ocarm.org, http://ocarm.org/en/content/ocarm/teresa-avila-quotes (Accessed December 12, 2017).

[7] *The Catechism of the Catholic Church*, para. 1638.

[8] Augustine of Hippo, "Sermons of St. Augustine of Hippo," *The Faith of The Early Fathers*, ed. William A. Jurgens, Vol. 3 (Collegeville: The Liturgical Press, 1979), para. 1498 [43,1], 26.

[9] Aquinas, *Summa Theologica* IIa-IIæ, Q. 1, Art. 5, reply obj. 1

[10] G. K. Chesterton, "The Red Angel," *Tremendous Trifles* (Pantianos Classics, 1909), 39.

[11] John Paul II, "MESSAGE OF THE HOLY FATHER JOHN PAUL II TO THE YOUTH OF THE WORLD ON THE OCCASION OF THE XIX WORLD YOUTH DAY 2004," para. 4, Vatican.va, https://w2.vatican.va/content/john-paul-ii/en/messages/youth/documents/hf_jp-ii_mes_20040301_xix-world-youth-day.html (Accessed December 21, 2017).

[12] Therese of Lisieux, *The Story of a Soul* (Rockford: Tan Books and Publishers, Inc., 1997), 153.

[13] *The Catechism of the Catholic Church*, para. 1829.

[14] Josemaria Escriva, *Conversations with Saint Josemaria Escriva* (New York: Scepter Publishers, Inc., 1968), no. 93, 144.

[15] Gwen Costello, *Spiritual Gems From Mother Teresa* (New London: Twenty-Third Publications, 2008), 11.

[16] Stephen Mark Holmes, "Homily by St. Gregory the Great, Fifteenth Sunday in Ordinary time/Proper 10 Year A: Matthew 13:1-23 or 13:1-9," *The Fathers on the Sunday Gospels* (Collegeville: Liturgical Press, 2012), 201.

CPSIA information can be obtained
at www.ICGtesting.com
Printed in the USA
FSHW020117301018
53281FS

9 781732 541108